VOLUME 2 **THE CITY OF OWLS**

BATMAN
VOLUME 2
THE CITY OF OWLS

SCOTT **SNYDER** writer

JAMES **TYNION IV** co-writer

GREG **CAPULLO** JONATHAN **GLAPION**
RAFAEL **ALBUQUERQUE** JASON **FABOK** BECKY **CLOONAN**
ANDY **CLARKE** SANDU **FLOREA** artists

FCO **PLASCENCIA** DAVE **McCAIG**
PETER **STEIGERWALD**
NATHAN **FAIRBAIRN** colorists

RICHARD **STARKINGS** COMICRAFT'S JIMMY **BETANCOURT**
SAL **CIPRIANO** DEZI **SIENTY** PATRICK **BROSSEAU** letterers

GREG **CAPULLO** & FCO **PLASCENCIA** cover artists

BATMAN created by BOB **KANE**

MIKE MARTS Editor – Original Series KATIE KUBERT Assistant Editor – Original Series PETER HAMBOUSSI Editor
ROBBIN BROSTERMAN Design Director – Books ROBBIE BIEDERMAN Publication Design

BOB HARRAS Senior VP – Editor-in-Chief, DC Comics

DIANE NELSON President DAN DIDIO and JIM LEE Co-Publishers
GEOFF JOHNS Chief Creative Officer
JOHN ROOD Executive VP – Sales, Marketing and Business Development
AMY GENKINS Senior VP – Business and Legal Affairs NAIRI GARDINER Senior VP – Finance
JEFF BOISON VP – Publishing Planning MARK CHIARELLO VP – Art Direction and Design
JOHN CUNNINGHAM VP – Marketing TERRI CUNNINGHAM VP – Editorial Administration
ALISON GILL Senior VP – Manufacturing and Operations HANK KANALZ Senior VP – Vertigo & Integrated Publishing
JAY KOGAN VP – Business and Legal Affairs, Publishing JACK MAHAN VP – Business Affairs, Talent
NICK NAPOLITANO VP – Manufacturing Administration SUE POHJA VP – Book Sales
COURTNEY SIMMONS Senior VP – Publicity BOB WAYNE Senior VP – Sales

BATMAN VOLUME 2: THE CITY OF OWLS

DC Comics, 1700 Broadway, New York, NY 10019
A Warner Bros. Entertainment Company
Printed by RR Donnelley, Salem, VA, USA. 4/26/13. Second Printing.

HC ISBN: 978-1-4012-3777-6
SC ISBN: 978-1-4012-3778-3

Library of Congress Cataloging-in-Publication Data

Snyder, Scott, author.
Batman. Volume 2, The City of Owls / Scott Snyder, Greg Capullo, Jonathan [sic] Glapion,
James Tynion IV, Rafael Albuquerque, Jason Fabok. pages cm
"Originally published in single magazine form in Batman 8-12, Batman Annual 1."
ISBN 978-1-4012-3777-6
1. Graphic novels. I. Capullo, Greg, illustrator. II. Glapion, Jonathan, illustrator. III. Tynion, James, IV, author. IV. Albuquerque, Rafael,
1981- illustrator. V. Fabok, Jay, illustrator. VI. Title. VII. Title: City of Owls.
PN6728.B36S683 2013
741.5'973—dc23
2012045985

 SUSTAINABLE
FORESTRY
INITIATIVE
Certified Chain of Custody
At Least 20% Certified Forest Content
www.sfiprogram.org
SFI-01042
APPLIES TO TEXT STOCK ONLY

Batman had believed the Court of Owls was just a nursery rhyme. As a young boy, he'd even honed his detective skills trying to prove that they existed, but never found any proof that a secret, owl-obsessed cabal ruled Gotham City.

That was before the Talon, the Court's legendary assassin, tried to kill Bruce Wayne in the middle of his meeting with mayoral candidate Lincoln March. It took all of his wits and skills as the Dark Knight to survive the deadly plummet from the top of Old Wayne Tower.

Batman uncovered the Court's nests, hidden in secret floors of Wayne-constructed buildings, dating as far back as the 19th century. The Talon then captured the Caped Crusader and proceeded to hunt the Dark Knight through a labyrinth for the Court's sadistic amusement!

While trapped in the Court's maze, Batman discovered evidence of a long-standing rivalry between the Owls and the Wayne family—proof that they were responsible for the death of his great-great-grandfather, architect Alan Wayne. After a strenuous battle with the Talon, Batman made a harrowing escape—almost at the cost of his own life.

In defeat, the Court abandoned their champion. Upon examining his bested enemy, Batman made several shocking discoveries. The Talon he'd fought was William Cobb, Dick Grayson's great-grandfather. The Court recruited their killers from Haly's Circus, and they had intended to make Dick their next executioner! Even more disconcerting was that the reanimation process had endowed Cobb with metahuman regenerative abilities, which only extreme cold could suppress.

Now, the Court has unleashed their ultimate offensive. They have awakened all of the previous generations' Talons from suspended animation and set them loose on Gotham City! **And their first stop is Wayne Manor...**

ATTACK ON WAYNE MANOR   SCOTT SNYDER writer   GREG CAPULLO penciller   JONATHAN GLAPION inker
THE CALL   SCOTT SNYDER & JAMES TYNION IV writers   RAFAEL ALBUQUERQUE artist
cover by GREG CAPULLO and FCO PLASCENCIA

I've always believed the best way to know the city is to stay close to the ground.

To feel the cracks in the sidewalk under your shoes.

The strange bright silence of the park under snow.

The hissing rain of sparks that comes down when the elevated train passes overhead on Third Avenue.

The late night ticking of traffic lights.

Because I know now that you can spend your whole life learning Gotham from deep inside...

It's only been in the last few weeks that I've come to understand how *wrong* I've been.

...and still know *nothing* about it at all.

...I'M A MAN STANDING OVER A *TOY CITY* HE MADE HIMSELF WHILE THE REAL ONE, THE ONE THAT *MATTERS,* OPERATES BEHIND HIS BACK.

I WASN'T TRADING IN WORDPLAY, SIR. YOU'VE BEEN SITTING IN THE DARK FOR HOURS.

AND YOU HAVE INFLAMMATION IN MOST OF THE TISSUE AROUND YOUR EYES AND A CONJUNCTIVAL HEMORRHAGE IN--

I'VE BEEN A FOOL, ALFRED.

AN ARROGANT *FOOL.*

PERHAPS. BUT THEN YOU COME FROM A *LONG LINE* OF SUCH MEN, SIR. AND THAT CITY ACROSS THE BAY IS A BETTER PLACE FOR ALL OF THEIR ARROGANT FOOLISHNESS.

ALFRED? DAMN.

WHAK

⸘UNH!⸘

CREAK...

HUH?

NO!

CLANG

YOUR LUCKY PENNY, SIR.

HEH. ARE YOU ALL RIGHT?

QUITE, SIR.

GOOD. NOW LET'S GET SOME ANSWERS.

"WE'RE COMING FOR YOU.

"YOU CAN'T STOP THE COURT.

"YOU CAN'T HOLD US BACK.

"THERE'S NOWHERE TO RUN ANYMORE.

"WE'RE IN THE HEART OF YOUR HOUSE, BRUCE! THE HOUSE OF WAYNE! AND OF BATMAN!"

THE ARMORY, ALFRED! GET INSIDE!

SIR--

QUICKLY!

THAT'S OKAY, BRUCE. WE'LL FIND A WAY IN.

WE ALWAYS DO.

NIGHT OF THE OWLS

SCOTT SNYDER writer **GREG CAPULLO** penciller **JONATHAN GLAPION** inker
cover by **GREG CAPULLO** and **FCO PLASCENCIA**

The first members of my family to live in the manor were *Solomon* and *Joshua Wayne*--brothers. They bought the house in 1855.

But they didn't move in until two years later.

The reason was *bats.*

A massive infestation of bats in the cave system beneath the land.

They brought in a chiroptologist from Gotham University, and according to him, to get rid of the bats, they'd have to introduce a *predator* into the cave.

So the Wayne brothers did.

They carted in all sorts of birds, from Peregrine Falcons to kestrels, and unleashed them in different sections of the cave.

The most effective killers of bats, though, were the *tiger owls.*

My ancestors let owls loose in the cave...

"Activate Fido."

WHUMP

GOOD BOY.

ARMORY
DOORS--

NO! OVERRIDE
ARMORY DOORS!
LOCK DOWN!

NO!
MASTER
BRUCE!

MASTER
BRUCE, YOU'RE
CRASHING!

My ancestors...
they used owls
to kill the bats.

Owls
everywhere.

But I forgot...
the thing I
forgot is...

...as soon as
the owls left...

...the bats...

...came back.

SIR, IT'S NEGATIVE TWENTY AND DROPPING.

THE TALONS SHOULD BE FEELING THE EFFECTS OF THE COLD BY NOW. BUT PLEASE, SIR, EXPOSED TO SUCH COLD, YOUR VITAL SIGNS--

THE COLD BROUGHT THE BATS OUT OF THE DARK, ALFRED.

I FEEL... FINE.

SIR, ONE OF THEM IS HEADED FOR THE BRIDGE, TRYING TO MAKE AN ESCAPE.

OH, I SEE HIM.

FIRST SNOW

SCOTT SNYDER & JAMES TYNION IV writers JASON FABOK artist
cover by JASON FABOK and PETER STEIGERWALD

AND WE HAVE UNTIL SUNSET TO BUILD OUR SNOWMAN, SILLY. THAT'S NEARLY TWO HOURS YET!

LOOK AROUND YOU--IT'S THE FIRST SNOW OF THE SEASON. YOU SHOULD *ENJOY* IT BEFORE IT'S MUDDIED.

BUT OUR SNOWMAN NEEDS TO BE *BIGGER* IF ALL WE'RE USING TO DECORATE HIM IS *THAT!*

SARAH AND PETRA, EVERYONE ELSE WILL BE USING ALL SORTS OF TRINKETS AND--

AND THEIR SNOWMEN WILL LOOK LIKE CLOWNS WITH RED LIPS AND BIRDS WITH LONG NOSES...

...*THIS* IS HOW WE DID IT IN THE OLD COUNTRY, AND HOW WE WILL DO IT HERE.

WE MAKE HIS FACE FROM THIS ONE *APPLE*...FROM OUR OWN TREE. FROM HIS EYES TO HIS WRINKLES.

THERE IS A CRAFT TO IT, VICTOR, AN ELEGANCE THAT SPEAKS OF *HOME.*

FINE, FINE. BUT WE'RE MAKING HIM *BIG*, JUST TO BE SAFE!

HA! ALL RIGHT THEN, WE WILL MAKE HIM AS BIG AS *YOU!*

I MEAN *BIGGER* THAN ME!

SO BIG HE WILL LAST THROUGH SPRING...

...BEFORE HE...

...MELTS?

VICTOR...

...IS THIS ANY WAY TO TREAT YOUR *FRIENDS?*

WE COULD HAVE SET A MEET. I WAS EXPECTING YOUR CALL FROM THE MOMENT THE ARKHAM INCIDENT CAME ACROSS THE POLICE WIRES.

DO YOU REALIZE HOW MUCH THIS WILL *COST* ME?

WHAT AM I SUPPOSED TO TELL THE POLICE, WHO ARE NO DOUBT ONLY *MINUTES* BEHIND YOU?

THE PUBLIC ENJOYS ITS LITTLE NARRATIVES, MR. COBBLEPOT.

MOVE A FEW HUNDRED THOUSAND DOLLARS OF YOUR LEGITIMATE MONEY INTO ONE OF YOUR SECRET VAULTS AND REPORT A *ROBBERY.*

THEY WILL READILY ACCEPT IT AS AN EXTENSION OF MY PERCEIVED FETISHIZATION OF *ICE.*

"...VENGEANCE ON *BRUCE WAYNE*."

DR. VICTOR FRIES, I PRESENT TO YOU THE PRODIGAL SON, BRUCE WAYNE.

DR. FRIES RUNS THE SMALL CRYONICS LAB WE KEEP BENEATH THE LABORATORIES PROPER. FROZEN HEADS ABOUND.

DOCTOR, I'M GIVING MR. WAYNE A TOUR OF HIS KINGDOM, IF YOU WILL. HE ONLY RECENTLY *RETURNED* TO GOTHAM.

RIGHT. OF COURSE. YOU WERE VACATIONING, I TAKE IT?

THAT'S ONE WAY OF PUTTING IT. ISN'T THAT RIGHT, LUCIUS?

DR. FRIES, MR. WAYNE HAS BEEN OUT OF THE COUNTRY FOR QUITE SOME TIME.

FORGIVE ME. ADMITTEDLY, I DON'T GET OUT OF THE LABORATORY VERY OFTEN. I NOW RECALL SOMETHING IN THE LOCAL NEWS ABOUT IT. YOUR RETURN, I MEAN.

DON'T GIVE IT A SECOND THOUGHT, DOCTOR. FROM WHAT I HEAR, YOU'RE DOING IMPORTANT WORK DOWN HERE.

YES, YES WE ARE. THE ADVANCEMENTS WE'VE MADE IN THE *SLOW-HEATING PROCESS* OF CRYO-PRESERVED INDIVIDUALS--

SLOW-HEATING? LUCIUS, I THOUGHT THE LAB WAS SUPPOSED TO BE MOVING *AWAY* FROM CRYONICS, FROZEN MUMMIES AND ALL THAT, TOWARDS NEWER, MORE SPECIALIZED FIELDS. LIKE ORGAN VITRIFICATION.

IN FACT, WEREN'T WE SUPPOSED TO TRANSFER THE REST OF THESE OLD CRYO-PRESERVED BODIES HERE TO THE GOTHAM UNIVERSITY BIO-LAB?

I FEEL I WAS PRETTY DIRECT IN SAYING I WASN'T COMFORTABLE CONTINUING WITH THIS LINE OF RESEARCH.

MR. WAYNE, WE CAN DO *BOTH!* WE CAN PURSUE NEW FIELDS LIKE VITRIFICATION WHILE STILL PURSU-ING OUR ORIGINAL RESEARCH ON THE REANIMATION OF CRYO-PRESERVED INDIVIDUALS.

BOTH...WELL, BE CAREFUL, DOCTOR. AND KNOW THAT YOU'LL BE UNDER *CLOSE EXAMINATION* UNTIL WE DECIDE WHAT TO DO WITH YOUR PROJECTS DOWN HERE.

MY NORA...DON'T WORRY. THEY WON'T TAKE YOU AWAY FROM ME.

I WON'T *LET* THEM.

NOT UNTIL I'VE FOUND A WAY TO BRING YOU *BACK*.

THERE IS A *CURE* FOR YOUR HEART NOW, MY LOVE. A NEWLY DEVELOPED OPERATION. ALL THAT REMAINS IS TO BRING YOU BACK TO ME. AND I'M CLOSE, NORA. *VERY CLOSE.*

FOR SO LONG, THE COLD HAS KEPT YOU, HELD YOU FAST. BUT SOON I WILL WAKE YOU FROM YOUR SLEEP LIKE A QUEEN IN A STORYBOOK...

VICTOR, IT'S *BRUCE WAYNE.* LET THE BOY GO.

WAYNE. SHOW YOUR FACE!

TAKE THE ELEVATOR UP TO THE PENTHOUSE, VICTOR. WE CAN STILL TALK THIS THROUGH. MAN TO MAN.

I GUARANTEE YOU, MR. WAYNE...

...*TALKING* IS NOT ON THE AGENDA.

WHAT ARE YOU DOING? GO *AFTER* HIM, YOU *IDIOT!*

CALM DOWN, ROBIN... BATMAN WANTS TO SETTLE THIS DIRECTLY. JUST THE TWO OF THEM.

"IT'S TIME, NORA. TIME FOR US TO BE *TOGETHER*..."

...I'VE WAITED SO LONG.

BUT THIS--THIS *NEW COMPOUND* IS EVERYTHING WE'VE BEEN WAITING FOR, MY LOVE.

AND IT WILL WORK. I *WILL* BRING YOU BACK.

NO, VICTOR...

...YOU WON'T.

MR. WAYNE! YOU DON'T UNDERSTAND. THIS IS NORA, MY WIFE, AND--

I UNDERSTAND *PERFECTLY*, DR. FRIES. I SHUT THIS PROJECT DOWN MONTHS AGO, AND YET YOU'VE CONTINUED TO WORK ON YOUR OWN *PRIVATE EXPERIMENTS*.

YOUR METHODS HERE HAVEN'T BEEN REVIEWED OR TESTED, AND YOU'RE ABOUT TO ADMINISTER THEM ON A *PERSON* WHO HAS NO MEANS OF CONSENT.

I *CAN'T* ALLOW YOU TO CONTINUE PLAYING MAD SCIENTIST WHILE YOU NEGLECT THE RESEARCH YOU WERE HIRED TO DO.

PLEASE, YOU MUST UNDER-STAND. MY NORA... SHE'S THE ONLY WOMAN I HAVE EVER LOVED.

AND HER CONDITION, THERE ARE SURGERIES NOW... PROCEDURES DEVELOPED SINCE SHE WAS FROZEN THAT COULD REPAIR HER HEART.

IT'S ALL FOR *HER*, MR. WAYNE. *PLEASE* LET ME CONTINUE.

NO, VICTOR. I'VE CALLED THE AUTHORITIES.

BUT SHE'S...NO. YOU *CAN'T!* YOU CAN'T TAKE HER FROM ME!

I CAN, AND I *WILL*. SHE'S STAYING HERE. AND YOU'RE GOING.

NO!

VICTOR, GET OUT OF THE WAY!

AAAHHH!

NOOO.... RRRAA. NORA...

"THIS IS INCREDIBLE, I'VE NEVER SEEN ANYTHING LIKE IT."

CSSSH

MY NORA...I HAVE CREATED THE PERFECT FORMULA, AND THOSE DAMN OWLS EVEN *TESTED* IT FOR US.

YOU'LL BE IN MY ARMS SOON ENOUGH, AS WE STAND OVER WAYNE'S CORPSE--

MR. WAYNE IS FAR AWAY. SAFE FROM YOU.

SOON NORA WILL BE, TOO.

HER NAME WAS *NORA FIELDS*, AND SHE WAS BORN IN 1943.

SHE WAS DIAGNOSED WITH AN INCURABLE HEART CONDITION WHEN SHE WAS TWENTY-THREE YEARS OLD. SHE HAD JUST GRADUATED FROM COLLEGE.

SHE WAS ENGAGED TO BE MARRIED TO A YOUNG LAWYER WHEN IT HAPPENED.

HER FAMILY DECIDED TO PUT HER UNDER A NEW AND CONTROVERSIAL TREATMENT, WHERE ONE DAY SHE MIGHT AWAKEN AND FIND A *NEW LIFE* IN A FUTURE WHERE SHE WOULDN'T HAVE TO DIE AT AGE TWENTY-FIVE.

SHE WAS THE *FIRST* PERSON TO UNDERGO *CRYOGENIC STASIS*, VICTOR. YOU WROTE YOUR DOCTORAL THESIS ON HER OVER A DECADE AGO.

THE CHANCE TO STUDY HER WAS THE ENTIRE REASON YOU CAME TO WORK AT WAYNE INDUSTRIES. SHE'S BEEN IN THIS BUILDING FOR *YEARS.*

"YOU NEVER KNEW HER, AND YET YOU COME BACK, TIME AND TIME AGAIN.

"*MR. FREEZE* OUT TO SAVE HIS DYING WIFE FROM THE CRUEL BUSINESSMAN WHO TOOK HER AWAY.

"BUT WE BOTH KNOW THAT'S A *FARCE*, VICTOR. SHE'S OLD ENOUGH TO BE YOUR GRANDMOTHER, FOR GOD'S SAKE."

...BEFORE IT'S *RUINED* BY FOOTPRINTS.

WE'RE OFF TO THE SNOWMAN CONTEST AGAIN, AREN'T WE, VICTOR?

YES, MOTHER.

BUT WHERE IS OUR APPLE? I FORGOT IT.

IT'S OKAY, MOTHER, WE CAN GET ONE THERE.

OH, SILLY ME... I GET SO CONFUSED SOMETIMES, EVER SINCE THAT ACCIDENT. WHAT ACCIDENT WAS IT, VICTOR?

NEVER MIND. I FOUND IT!

I HAVE OUR APPLE RIGHT *HERE!*

I ALREADY *CARVED* IT, TOO! YOU SEE, VICTOR?

I SEE, MOTHER.

NOW REST.

...ri Ducard, the great detective, ...e told me that there's a feeling ...get on a case sometimes...

Earlier tonight, when Lincoln March gave me his short list of names, I felt it. I saw Joseph Powers' name on the list and I *knew.*

Not just because he was responsible for the founding of the Gotham Aviary, for its exceptional collection of rare owls. Not because his finances seem *skewed.* But because I felt it in my gut, that *remembering.*

And now, here, I feel it again...

...eling that comes when ...eces suddenly fit into ...and the answer you've ...ooking for all that ...egins to appear.

The feeling, Ducard said, is like "a remembering." Not so much a discovery of something new, as a remembering of what you knew all along. Something right in front of you.

...eeling is the best ...or you have your ..., said Ducard.

...outside this building.

I came to *Harbor House* when I was a boy. I was looking for the Court of Owls.

That time I found nothing.

Not tonight.

Tonight, the Court goes down. Once and for all.

No more hiding. No more plotting from the shadows.

Tonight their story **ends**. Their little song will be forgotten. Their name vanishes from Gotham's history.

They know it, too. Rushing to meet here in the middle of the night.

The report from Alfred is that many of the assassination attempts tonight were stopped. Most of the Court's Talons are down.

And now I have them cornered.

No security, no traps...**nothing** can keep me from them.

"...DAMN YOU *ALL*."

MASTER BRUCE?

YOU'RE NOT DRESSED. DON'T FORGET, YOU'RE MEETING WITH THE FIRMS BIDDING ON THE ELEVATED PARK IN LESS THAN AN HOUR.

I TOLD YOU. I'M WAITING ON THE GRAY, ALFRED.

YES, WELL, IT SEEMS TO HAVE SNUCK UP ON YOU, SIR.

IT DOESN'T *MAKE SENSE,* ALFRED. MEMBERS OF THE COURT, TAKING THEIR OWN LIVES, JUST LIKE THAT.

SO WHY DON'T YOU GIVE ME THOSE MORBID THINGS SO I MAY RETURN THEM TO THEIR CASE, AND YOU CAN START THINKING ABOUT TREES AND PONDS AND A GREENER CITY.

I RATHER THINK IT *DOES,* SIR. YOU'VE TAKEN THE CITY BACK FROM THEM.

THEN THERE'S THE MONEY. MONEY SIPHONED FROM THE DEAD MEMBERS' ACCOUNTS IN JUST THE LAST FEW WEEKS...IT FEELS MORE LIKE A SETUP. LIKE SUBTERFUGE.

YOU SAW THE AUTOPSIES, MASTER BRUCE. THE COURT MEMBERS ARE *QUITE DEAD.*

SOMETHING DOESN'T FIT ABOUT IT, ALFRED. THERE'S SOMETHING BEHIND IT. I CAN *FEEL* IT. SOMEONE CLOSE. CLOSE ALL ALONG.

THAT MAY BE, SIR. BUT THE ANSWERS WILL COME. YOU NOW KNOW THE IDENTITIES OF AT LEAST *SEVERAL* OF THE COURT OF OWLS' MAJOR FIGUREHEADS.

AND WHILE THEIR ORGANIZATION, AS YOU'VE DISCOVERED, IS CLEARLY MUCH *LARGER* THAN THIS ONE GROUPING, I'M CERTAIN YOU'LL EVENTUALLY BRING THEM ALL TO JUSTICE.

IF I MAY SPEAK FREELY, SIR, PERHAPS THE THING THAT DOESN'T FIT ABOUT THIS ENDING IS THAT IT *IS* AN ENDING.

I KNOW WHEN YOU WERE A BOY YOU THOUGHT YOU MIGHT FIND ANSWERS TO YOUR PARENTS' MURDER IN THE COURT OF OWLS, AND MY SUSPICION IS THAT PERHAPS YOU WERE HOPING YOU MIGHT FIND MORE ANSWERS *NOW.*

WHAT GAVE YOU THAT IDEA?

WHEN IT COMES TO THEM? TO THEIR MURDER? *YOU* ARE THE ANSWER TO THAT MYSTERY, BRUCE WAYNE. AND *THAT* ANSWER...

...IS ENOUGH.

NOW PUT ON THAT BLOODY SUIT AND GET OUT OF HERE!

ALL RIGHT, ALL RIGHT. I'M GOING.

JUST CALL ROBERTS AND TELL...

...TELL HIM...

TELL HIM *WHAT*, SIR?

TELL HIM...

...I WON'T BE ABLE TO MAKE IT.

BUT, SIR. WHERE ARE YOU--

I'M GOING AFTER HIM, ALFRED.

Sinkholes are tricky things. They can form in more places than most people think.

In cities, they form particularly quickly, often exacerbated by leaky pipes and overly heavy structures.

Gotham has a sinkhole. Just one. It's the only one in Kane County, in fact.

And it sits beneath this place.

The Willowwood Home for Children.

Years ago, it was Gotham's satellite hospital for children suffering from mental illness and neurological disorders.

It operated until eighteen years ago, when a sinkhole swallowed the orderlies' quarters.

In the days that followed the catastrophe, the truth about Willowwood became clear.

The abuses the children had been subjected to. The neglect. Children. Alone, naked, rotting in their filth. Left to starve.

Now, it sits abandoned, and children dare each other to spend the night inside.

They say the sadness of the lost children caused the sinkhole. They say the place is haunted by their spirits.

Tonight, I almost believe it...after all, I'm here to catch a dead man.

I'M HERE.

‡UNH!‡

SO TELL ME, BATMAN... *WHO?*

WHO *AM I?*

I DON'T KNOW. BUT YOU'RE NOT LINCOLN MARCH. BECAUSE LINCOLN MARCH *DOESN'T EXIST.*

HE'S A PAPER MAN, SET UP BY THE COURT OF OWLS.

GOOD. SO IF I'M NOT LINCOLN MARCH, THEN WHO AM I?

THE PIN.

THE *PIN!* WHAT PIN?

IN THE STORY YOU TOLD ME, IN OLD WAYNE TOWER. ABOUT YOUR MOTHER'S DEATH. THE CAR ACCIDENT THAT KILLED HER.

THERE'S THE LIE, BUT WHERE'S THE *TRUTH?*

YOU MENTIONED A *PIN* SHE WORE. A MISSHAPEN HEART PIN. MADE OF CLAY.

AND?

"YOU SAW THE PICTURE OF *MY MOTHER* WEARING THAT PIN AND YOU USED IT IN YOUR--"

NO. THE TRUTH IN THE LIE, BRUCE. THAT PIN. IT WAS ONLY GIVEN TO THE MOTHERS OF CHILDREN WHO LIVED HERE AT WILLOWWOOD.

SO WHO AM I, BRUCE?

WHO? I ASK, LIKE THE GREAT OWL, *WHO?!*

YOU'RE SICK.

YOU'RE NOTHING. YOU'RE--

YOUR *BROTHER,* BRUCE.

I'M *THOMAS WAYNE, JR.*

YOUR BROTHER THAT *NEVER WAS.* FROM THE OTHER SIDE OF THE MIRROR.

I DON'T HAVE A BROTHER!

OH, BUT YOU WERE *SUPPOSED* TO, THOUGH, REMEMBER? I KNOW YOU DO. THINK BACK, TO BEFORE. I WAS THERE, IN MOTHER'S STOMACH... BUT THERE WAS AN *ACCIDENT,* BRUCE. REMEMBER?

YOU WERE *THERE.* I WAS BORN EARLY, BORN HURT. AND OUR PARENTS *HID* ME HERE. AT *WILLOWWOOD.* TO HEAL AWAY FROM THE WORLD.

I DON'T KNOW WHAT THE HELL YOU'RE TALKING ABOUT, LINCOLN, WHAT STORY THE COURT *CONCOCTED* FOR YOU, BUT THAT'S *THEIR* MISTAKE.

MY PARENTS WOULDN'T DO THAT. THEY WOULDN'T PUT A SON OF THEIRS, SICK OR NOT, IN A PLACE LIKE *THIS.*

SEE, BUT IT WASN'T LIKE THIS BACK THEN, AT THE TIME OF THE ACCIDENT. IT WAS A *PREMIER* CHILDREN'S HOSPITAL.

THAT IS UNTIL THE FUNDING DRIED UP. WHEN THE HOSPITAL'S BIGGEST DONORS DIED. THOMAS AND MARTHA WAYNE. TRAGICALLY *SHOT IN AN ALLEY.*

YOU WANTED TO KNOW IF THE COURT HAD ANYTHING TO DO WITH OUR PARENTS' DEATHS, BRUCE. THE ANSWER IS *NO.* THEY DIDN'T. THAT WAS ALL *YOUR FAULT,* BROTHER.

AND I'M GOING TO MAKE YOU PAY.

SO FINISH CUTTING THROUGH THE NET. AND LET'S HAVE THIS OUT ONCE AND FOR ALL... FOR THE *CITY OF GOTHAM.*

WAYNE TO WAYNE.

YOU'RE OUT OF YOUR MIND...

BROTHER TO BROTHER...

MY BROTHER'S KEEPER SCOTT SNYDER writer GREG CAPULLO penciller JONATHAN GLAPION inker
THE FALL OF THE HOUSE OF WAYNE SCOTT SNYDER & JAMES TYNION IV writers RAFAEL ALBUQUERQUE artist
cover by GREG CAPULLO

WELL, THIS TIME THE STORY HAS A *TWIST ENDING*, BRUCE! BECAUSE THIS TIME THE FALLEN BROTHER *WINS* IN THE END!

ALL RIGHT, LINCOLN...

...YOU WANT TO BE MY FALLEN BROTHER SO BAD...

...THEN START FALLING!

...WELCOME TO THE OTHER SIDE OF THE *MIRROR*, BRUCE!

NOW LIVE AS *I* DID! RIGHT FROM THE START!

FEEL YOURSELF BEING *BORN AGAIN* AS ME IN THAT CAR CRASH. YOU'RE LIKE A BIRD DROPPED FROM THE NEST, SMASHED AWAKE!

NOW YOU'RE A CHILD, YOU'RE GROWING, BUT YOU'RE BROKEN. SOMETHING IS *WRONG*. YOU CAN'T MOVE, CAN'T TALK.

YOU CAN *SEE*, THOUGH, THROUGH THE BAREST OF SLITS BETWEEN YOUR EYELIDS...YOU *WATCH*.

EVERYONE THINKS YOU'RE *ASLEEP* INSIDE. THEY'RE WAITING FOR YOU TO *DIE*... EVERY DAY YOU'RE SUPPOSED TO! BUT YOU DON'T...

...BECAUSE YOU'RE ALIVE IN THERE! YOU'RE *AWAKE*! YOU DON'T EVEN KNOW WHO YOU ARE, BUT YOU'RE SOMEONE! YOU *FEEL* IT!

WHO, THOUGH? *WHO*?

AND THERE'S THE WOMAN. SHE COMES OFTEN. SHE SITS ON YOUR BED. YOU KNOW SHE'S YOUR *MOTHER*, SHE'S THE *KEY*!

BUT YOU CAN'T CALL TO HER, CAN'T MOVE!

AND THEN ONE DAY, SHE'S ON THE TELEVISION IN YOUR ROOM. AND YOU *KNOW!*

A *REVELATION!* SUDDENLY YOU KNOW WHO YOU *ARE*, BECAUSE THE OWLS ARE THERE NOW, TOO. *WHISPERING* TO YOU AT NIGHT.

TELLING YOU WHAT YOU *ALREADY KNEW* ALL ALONG-- THAT YOU'RE *THOMAS WAYNE, JR.* A SON OF THE CITY!

YOUR PARENTS ARE GONE, BUT YOUR BROTHER! YOUR *BROTHER* IS STILL OUT THERE!

AND YOU THINK TO YOURSELF, *HE'LL* COME FOR ME, WON'T HE? HE'LL COME FOR ME...

YOU WAIT EVERY DAY, ALL DAY, THE OWLS WHISPERING AS THE HOUSE AROUND YOU GOES TO HELL.

BUT HE DOESN'T COME. ONLY THE *OWLS* COME, AND SOON ENOUGH, THEY SAVE YOU FROM THAT PLACE, THEY START TO HELP YOU HEAL, FIX YOUR MIND.

STILL YOU WAIT FOR YOUR BROTHER... HE *MUST* REMEMBER YOU! YOU KNOW HE DOES! BUT ALL YOU HEAR IS THE TIME PASSING. THE BIG CHURCH BELL RINGING... *BONG! BONG! BONG!*

BONG

IT'S OKAY, BRUCE! YOU CAN *LET GO* NOW!

YOUR BROTHER IS WATCHING OVER YOU. JUST AS HE *ALWAYS* HAS.

Suit...
dead.

Nothing left.
No power.

Can't hold on
any longer...

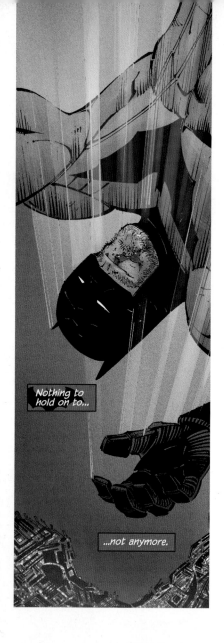

Nothing to hold on to...

...not anymore.

She looks so beautiful from up here.

Dick...you always liked taking the plane.

Seeing the city this way...

...I see why.

I try to let go...

...but even as I do...

...the city...

...she calls me back to her.

She saves me.

She reminds me...we still have work to do.

SWITCH TO HIGH VELOCITY BAT-ROPE, NOW!

YOU'D BEEN GONE FOR YEARS. YOU'D LEFT TO TRAVEL THE WORLD...

...AND YOU *DISAPPEARED.* THE COURT HAD SAID YOU DIED SOMEWHERE IN THE HIMALAYAS, OR THE BACK ALLEYS OF PARIS.

I WAS HEALED, AND THE OWLS' PLAN WAS TO PRESENT ME TO THE CITY AS MYSELF, AS *THOMAS WAYNE, JR.* I WAS GOING TO BRING THE HOUSE OF WAYNE TO ITS GREATEST HEIGHTS, WITH THEIR HELP.

BUT THEN... YOU *RETURNED.* OUT OF NOWHERE.

AND THE COURT THOUGHT THE SPOTLIGHT ON THE WAYNE FAMILY WAS TOO BRIGHT...

SO THEY CAME UP WITH *"LINCOLN MARCH."* A MAN I COULD BECOME TO RECLAIM THE CITY FOR THEM IN A DIFFERENT WAY. *"YOU'LL BE THE BEAK OF THE GREAT OWL,"* THEY SAID.

BUT THAT'S NOT WHAT I WANTED, BRUCE. I WANTED THE CITY IN EARNEST. IT WAS *MY TIME.*

NOW I CAN *NEVER* HAVE IT. I KNOW THAT. BUT IF I CAN'T BE THIS CITY'S FUTURE, I'LL BE ITS *SECRET PAST...*

...I'LL BE THE PAST COME TO GET YOU. THE GOTHAM OF THE DEAD, THE *GHOST CITY.* ALL THE ONES YOU NEVER LOOKED BACK AT IN YOUR ARROGANCE. I'LL STAND FOR THEM.

SO DIE KNOWING THIS, BROTHER. YOU? YOU'RE NOTHING BUT A *FOOTNOTE,* A *BLIP,* DESTINED TO BE *FORGOTTEN.*

ME, I *AM* GOTHAM'S HISTORY!

FINALLY ≥KOFF≤...

"THE WHOLE TOWER WAS DESTROYED, DOWN TO ITS FOUNDATION.

"I CONDUCTED A SEARCH PRIVATELY AND CAME UP EMPTY, TOO.

"NO CASUALTIES.

"NO BODIES FOUND IN THE WRECKAGE AT ALL."

"IM STILL MAKING INROADS, FOLLOWING THE MONEY. BUT THE TRUTH IS, THEIR RESOURCES ARE *STAGGERING.* AND THE MAZE THEY'VE MADE TO HIDE THEIR TRAIL...WITHOUT A DOUBT, THEY'RE STILL OUT THERE...

"...BUT THEY'RE HURTING. AND I'LL MAKE SURE THEY *KEEP* HURTING UNTIL I FIND THEM ALL...

"...AND WASH AWAY THE STAIN OF THE COURT ALTOGETHER."

"AND THE CAPTURED TALONS?"

"I'VE HAD THEM MOVED TO A CRYO-PRISON BENEATH BLACKGATE. WAYNE FUNDED, OF COURSE.

"AS FOR THE ONES WHO GOT AWAY, WE'LL FIND THEM SOON ENOUGH."

OF COURSE WE WILL. JUST A MATTER OF TIME.

I'LL BE SEEING YOU, BRUCE.

DICK, WAIT...

I ASSUME ALFRED TOLD YOU ABOUT LINCOLN MARCH'S CLAIMS?

HE DID. BUT WITH HOW THINGS HAVE BEEN BETWEEN US LATELY...HONESTLY, I DIDN'T WANT TO PRY.

NO. I'D LIKE YOU TO KNOW.

THERE *WAS* ANOTHER WAYNE CHILD...

...I WAS THREE WHEN MY MOTHER WAS PREGNANT WITH...HIM. WE WERE IN A CAR ACCIDENT TOGETHER. I DON'T...I DON'T REMEMBER THE ACCIDENT. BUT THERE'S A RECORD.

THE CHILD WAS BORN PREMATURE, WITH NEUROLOGICAL DAMAGE. SEVERE ENOUGH THAT HE WOULD HAVE REMAINED IN A PERMANENT VEGETATIVE STATE HAD HE LIVED THROUGH THE INITIAL TRAUMA.

HE DIDN'T LIVE, THOUGH?

HE DID...

...FOR A SINGLE NIGHT.

AND YOU'RE ALL RIGHT WITH THAT?

NO. I'M NOT. BUT I SUPPOSE IN THIS CITY I *HAVE* TO BE.

WELL THAT'S VERY BIG OF Y--

UNTIL I FIND THAT EVIDENCE.

THE COURT OF OWLS TRIED TO UNDERMINE EVERYTHING I BELIEVE IN, BUT ONE THING THEY COULD NEVER MAKE ME QUESTION IS MY BELIEF IN MY PARENTS. IF THOMAS, JR. HAD LIVED PAST THAT ONE NIGHT, THEY'D HAVE *TOLD* ME.

THEY WOULD HAVE. I KNOW IT.

I BELIEVE WHAT YOU BELIEVE, BRUCE. BUT STILL...

IF THOMAS WAS NEVER SUPPOSED TO RECOVER, I MEAN IF IT WAS HOPELESS...

LOOK, ALL I'M SAYING IS THAT SOMETIMES, PROTECTING THE PEOP[LE] YOU CARE ABOUT FROM PAINFUL TRUTH AND CARRYING IT AS A PRIV[ATE] PAIN INSTEAD...I NOW SEE THAT IT CAN BE A *NOBLE* THING, YOU KNOW?

...

DICK, LISTEN. I KNOW IT MUST HAVE BEEN HARD, FINDING OUT THAT YOU WERE MEANT TO BE A TALON, TO BE ONE OF THE OWLS.

WELL THANK YOU, B--

I'M NOT DONE.

I KNOW IT MIGHT SEEM LIKE I SAVED YOU FROM THAT DESTINY. BUT YOU COULD NEVER HAVE BEEN ONE OF THEM. *NEVER*. THEY MIGHT HAVE SEEN SOMETHING IN YOU, BACK THEN. BUT SO DID I.

AND THE TRUTH IS, I DIDN'T SAVE YOU FROM SOME DARK FATE, THOSE YEARS AGO. YOU SAVED [ME]...

AND YOU STILL ARE SAVING ME, EVERY DAY.

...

≥SIGH≤ DAMMIT, BRUCE. NOW I CAN'T HIT YOU. I'LL JUST HAVE TO DO IT SOME OTHER TIME. IT'S FINE, THOUGH. I'LL JUST SNEAK UP AND SURPRISE YOU.

YOU'LL TRY.

SO YOU GOING TO REBUILD?

THE TOWER? I AM. *TALLER.* IN FACT, I'M REDOUBLING MY EFFORTS WITH THE INITIATIVE.

WELL, IT'S NICE TO KNOW THAT THE OWLS DIDN'T SCARE BRUCE WAYNE BACK INTO HIS CAVE.

THE OPPOSITE, ACTUALLY. IT'S STRANGE, DICK. LATELY, RIGHT UP UNTIL ALL THIS WITH THE COURT, I'D COME TO THINK OF THE CITY AS MINE. AS BATMAN'S.

EVEN WITH THE INITIATIVE, PART OF ME WAS DOING IT TO HAVE MORE LOOKOUTS. MORE BASES FOR BATMAN RATHER THAN FOR THE CITY ITSELF. BUT I SEE NOW THAT I WAS *WRONG.*

BECAUSE GOTHAM ISN'T BATMAN.

GOTHAM ISN'T THE OWLS.

GOTHAM IS...

GOTHAM IS *ALL* OF US.

IT'S A *LITTLE* BIT BATMAN. COME ON.

IN THE END, I HAVE TO SAY I'M GRATEFUL TO THE COURT OF OWLS FOR THE LESSON. BUT EVEN SO, IF THEY REEMERGE... *WHEN* THEY REEMERGE...

...that all of it was for you, Alfred.

For I was convinced that in doing my best to serve, to help in my own way to improve this home and this family, I was making a better future for you.

Especially when it came to young Master Wayne, whom I knew you would one day serve.

I loved and cared for him so that he would one day care for you.

At least this is what I believed, then...

...perhaps I was lying to myself, though, Alfred. Perhaps I simply lost myself in the happiness of those days. That young family.

But they were happy times, my Son. Know that, too.

...but the very legacy of the Wayne Family.

You see, Martha had resolved herself to the creation of a new school for Gotham's underprivileged, its forgotton children.

She believed that through this school, she could shape the city into something brighter for young Master Bruce...

...and for her second child, who was nearly due to be born.

I spent my days caring for Bruce as his mother tended to her plans and to her pregnancy.

Even at three years old, Bruce was an an exceptional child. Smart and kind...I knew you would love him one day as I do. But now, none of that will come to pass.

"JARVIS, CAN YOU COME IN HERE FOR A MOMENT?"

Martha's hope and purity of spirit pushed me to agree. But I knew, in my heart, I should have insisted that we stay home.

I had my suspicions, now, as to what figures haunted the Waynes.

The Owl in the window had sealed my dread.

I could hear that silly rhyme growing louder in the back of my head, the closer we got to the school grounds.

The closer we got to that damned intersection...

SKREEEEEEE

...on the corner of Lincoln and March.

Tonight, Alfred, the shadows haunting Wayne Manor have come for me.

My goal--my only goal--is to reach you, my dear Son. And hold you again. But...

...should we never meet again in this lifetime, remember these simple truths.

Remember my love for you. Forgive me for all my many fatherly sins and know I tried my hardest to create a better life for you.

And remember, please, to fear Gotham City. Never visit, even in the event of my passing. This is a cursed place, a place that tricks you into loving it, into hoping... and the Wayne grounds, they are the most unholy of all. These lovely grounds...

...but I must hurry. I trust that if I should die, this warning will reach you and keep you safe from harm.

for ALFRED

With deep love and regret,

Your father

Jarvis Pennyw...

GHOST IN THE MACHINE
SCOTT SNYDER & JAMES TYNION IV writers BECKY CLOONAN artist ANDY CLARKE additional art SANDU FLOREA additional inks
cover by GREG CAPULLO and FCO PLASCENCIA

Sometimes all it takes is a few words to change your life.

For me it took *seven*. Seven words, spoken in the dark.

I was at work when I heard them. Sixty feet below Gotham City, down deep...working on the eastern section of the old power grid.

I was on a stretch of cable that'd been eaten away by a drip of snow-melter salt. It was chomped through, frayed and sparking at 69,000 volts...

...when I heard those seven words...

HARPER, PHONECALL! YOUR BROTHER-- HE SOUNDS PISSED!

...no, not those.

MY BROTHER? WHAT THE HELL TIME IS IT, ANYWAY?

The words I'm talking about came later...

"...FIXING IT ISN'T WHAT I HAD IN MIND."

YOU ALL RIGHT, HOMO?

DEF, HOMO.

SEE YOU ON THE OTHER SIDE.

I guess you could say I grew up fixing things.

"EARTH TO HARPER?"

SHOULDN'T YOU BE ASLEEP?

WANT TO SEE SOMETHING COOL?

≥SIGH≤ YOU'VE SHOWN ME, LIKE, A *HUNDRED* VIDEOS OF BATMAN, AND NONE OF THEM HAVE BEEN EVEN *HALF* AS COOL AS SEEING HIM IN REAL LIFE. I MEAN, TRUST ME, I *GET* THE BAT-OBSESSION.

THE LAST FEW DAYS I'VE BEEN ABLE TO WALK HOME WITHOUT HAVING TO WORRY ABOUT ANYONE GIVING ME CRAP. I *LOVE* BATMAN...

...BUT YOU'VE BEEN ON YOUR COMPUTER WATCHING EVERY LITTLE SCRAP OF VIDEO YOU CAN FIND. DON'T YOU THINK IT'S TIME TO... I DON'T KNOW... GIVE IT A REST?

JUST SHUT UP AND CHECK THIS OUT. I NOTICED THAT ALL THE FOOTAGE OF BATMAN OUT THERE HAS COME FROM SMARTPHONES, CAMERAS... THE KINDS OF THINGS WHERE ALL YOU SEE IS JUST A *BLUR*. SO I THOUGHT I'D TAKE A CLOSER LOOK.

"...BECAUSE THE THING IS, THE GOTHAM GRID CAN'T BE ACCESSED REMOTELY THE WAY IT'S CONSTRUCTED.

"SO FOR BATMAN TO BE ABLE TO SHUT DOWN THINGS LIKE THIS, HE'D NEED TO HAVE HIS OWN NETWORK. SOME KIND OF *GHOST GRID* BUILT INTO THE SYSTEM, OR BENEATH IT.

"SOMETHING HE CAN ACCESS REMOTELY, TOO. I MEAN, IT'S NOT LIKE HE'S COMING DOWN TO THE SEWERS TO FLIP A SWITCH WHENEVER HE NEEDS TO.

"I ASKED MY BOSS WHAT IT WOULD TAKE TO *BUILD* SOMETHING LIKE THAT. A SORT OF PRIVATE GRID INSIDE THE GRID.

"AND HE SAID THE FIRST THING YOU'D NEED IS *POWER.* BECAUSE THE GRID ITSELF IS STRAINED TO CAPACITY. YOU RUN A SEPARATE SYSTEM OFF IT AND YOU'LL CRASH THE WHOLE THING.

"SO I RAN SOME LEVELS, AND WHAT I DISCOVERED IS THAT THERE'RE FIFTEEN SPOTS ON THE GRID--*HUBS* WHERE BATMAN COULD PENETRATE THE MAINFRAME AND SAP POWER.

"BUT THE FUNNY THING IS, HE ISN'T USING HIS GHOST GRID TO SCRAMBLE SIGNALS AND VIDEO AND ALL THAT. GET THIS...

"...HE'S ALSO USING HIS GRID TO HELP *SUSTAIN* THE GOTHAM ELECTRICAL GRID. HIS GRID IS HELPING PROP UP THE CITY'S. HE'S LIKE THE GHOST IN THE MACHINE.

"HE ACTUALLY SAPS POWER SECRETLY FROM WAYNE INDUSTRIES BUILDINGS, LIKE ROBIN HOOD, TO POWER THESE BOXES HE KEEPS AT THE HUBS. THEY'RE AMPLIFIERS...*BAT-BOXES.*

"THE BOXES ALSO HELP HIM GHOST *HIMSELF.*"

"WHOA, *WHOA.* YOU *FOUND* A BAT-BOX?"

I JUST WANTED TO DO SOMETHING TO HELP HIM OUT... HE'S USING STORE-BOUGHT WAYNE INDUSTRIES ANTENNAS TO BROADCAST HIS NETWORK...

...SO I COBBLED TOGETHER SOMETHING THAT'D GIVE EACH OF THE STATIONS MORE RANGE.

THAT WAY, IF ONE OF THE STATIONS EVER GOES DOWN, HE CAN STILL GET ACCESS TO THE GRID FROM ONE OF THE OTHER BOXES.

IT'S JUST A THANK-YOU, I GUESS. FOR EVERYTHING.

MAN, I WAS JUST THINKING ABOUT GETTING A BAT *TATTOOED* ON MY ARM OR SOMETHING, BUT YOU LEVELED UP.

BEEEEEP

OOH! HE'S IN THE CITY!

IN THE--? HARPER, ARE YOU... *TRACKING* BATMAN?

NO! I MEAN, MAYBE JUST A LITTLE. YOU CAN SEE THE RANGE OF EACH OF THE TOWERS HERE, AND THAT'S HOW BATMAN CAN MANIPULATE THE GRID...

...HE'S OVER BY THE DOCKS RIGHT NOW. NOT TOO FAR FROM HERE, ACTUALLY. AND AS LONG AS THESE STAY UP--

--WHAT THE...THIS ONE JUST WENT OFFLINE.

VARIANT COVER GALLERY

BATMAN 8
by Jason Fabok & Peter Steigerwald

BATMAN 9
by Dale Keown & FCO Plascencia

BATMAN 10
by Rafael Albuquerque

BATMAN 11
by Andy Clarke & Tomeu Morey

BATMAN 12
by Bryan Hitch & Nathan Fairbairn